Little Scientists BIG Questions?

Where Did All the Dinosaurs Go?

Dinosaurs lived on Earth

millions and
millions and . . .

MILLIONS AND MILLIONS

OF YEARS AGO!

4

But why are there no dinosaurs alive today?
Where did all the dinosaurs go?
Come on little scientists, let's answer those BIG questions!

In prehistoric times there were lots of different dinosaurs.

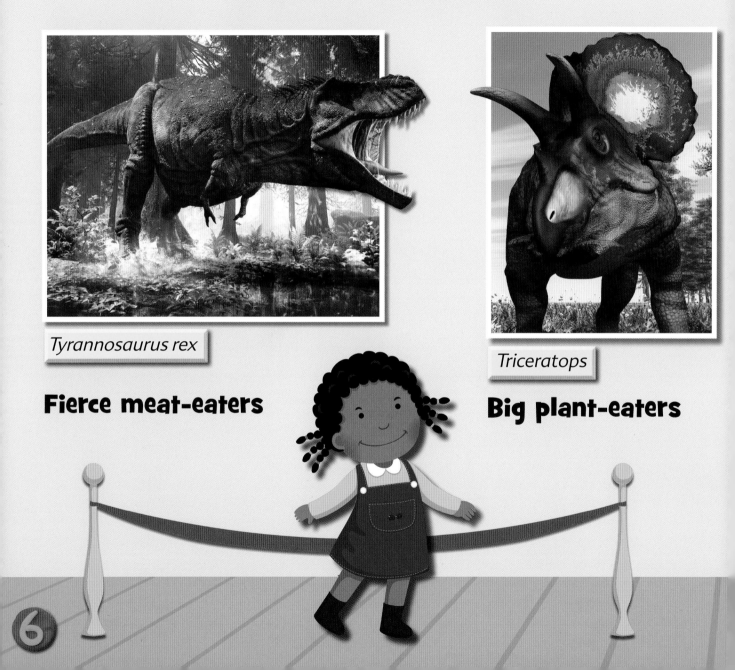

Tyrannosaurus rex

Fierce meat-eaters

Triceratops

Big plant-eaters

Then one day about 66 million years ago,
something **BAD** happened.

Something **VERY** bad.

A **giant** space rock called
an **asteroid** crashed
into **Earth.**

Get ready for some **BIG** science!

The asteroid caused fires and flooding.

Smoke, dust and ash filled the sky and blocked out the Sun.

Plants couldn't grow on the dark, burning land.

Plant-eating dinosaurs died because they had no food.

The meat-eating dinosaurs also died. Why? Because there were no plant-eaters to feed on.

Most of the dinosaurs on Earth died and were gone forever.

This is called going extinct.

Let's say it! "ex-TINK-t"

More BIG science coming up!

crocodile

Some dinosaurs and other prehistoric animals didn't die.

Crocodiles are relatives of dinosaurs. They **lived** at the same time as the **dinosaurs** and are still around **today.**

Some prehistoric animals changed and became the animals we know today.

It took millions of years, but some kinds of dinosaurs became birds!

hoatzin bird

The long-ago relatives of hoatzin birds were dinosaurs.

ROAR!

If the **dinosaurs** went **extinct** millions of years ago, how do we know they were here?

Sometimes, when a dinosaur died, it left behind **rocky clues.**

rocky dinosaur skeleton

An old dinosaur lay down by a river and died.

Other animals ate the **soft, meaty bits** of its body.

Soon, only **bones** were left.

The bones washed into the river.

They sank to the riverbed and were **buried in mud.**

Pssssttttt
Turn your book clockwise.

4 More and more layers of rock formed.

Great job!

What happened to the dinosaur's bones next?

1 More and more layers of mud covered the bones.

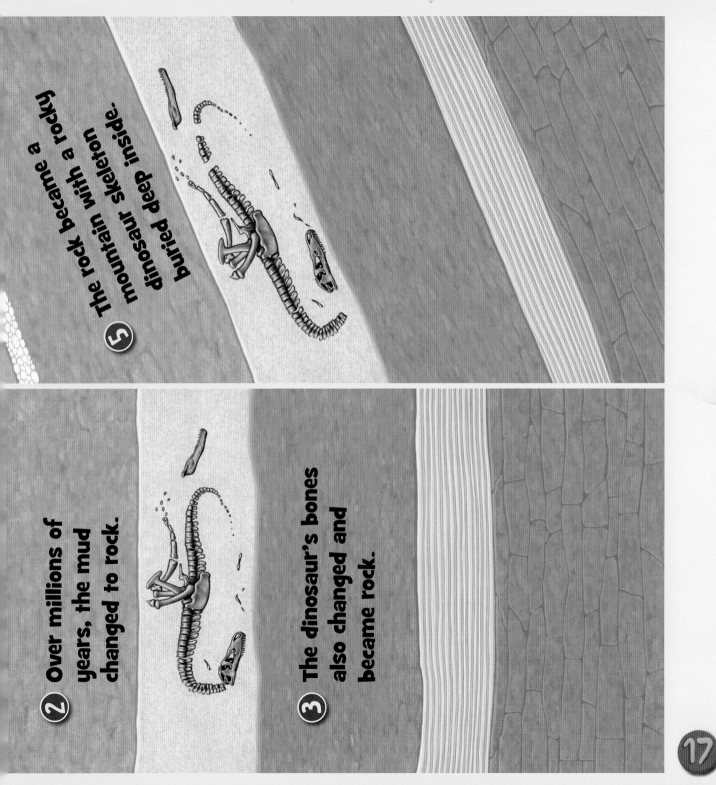

5 The rock became a rocky mountain with a rocky dinosaur skeleton buried deep inside.

2 Over millions of years, the mud changed to rock.

3 The dinosaur's bones also changed and became rock.

Turn your book again.

3 Rain and melted snow wash over the rock, making it crumble away.

1 Over millions of years the weather can change a mountain.

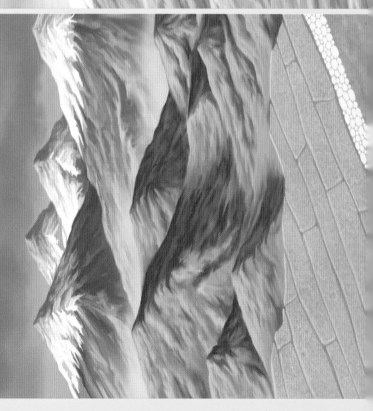

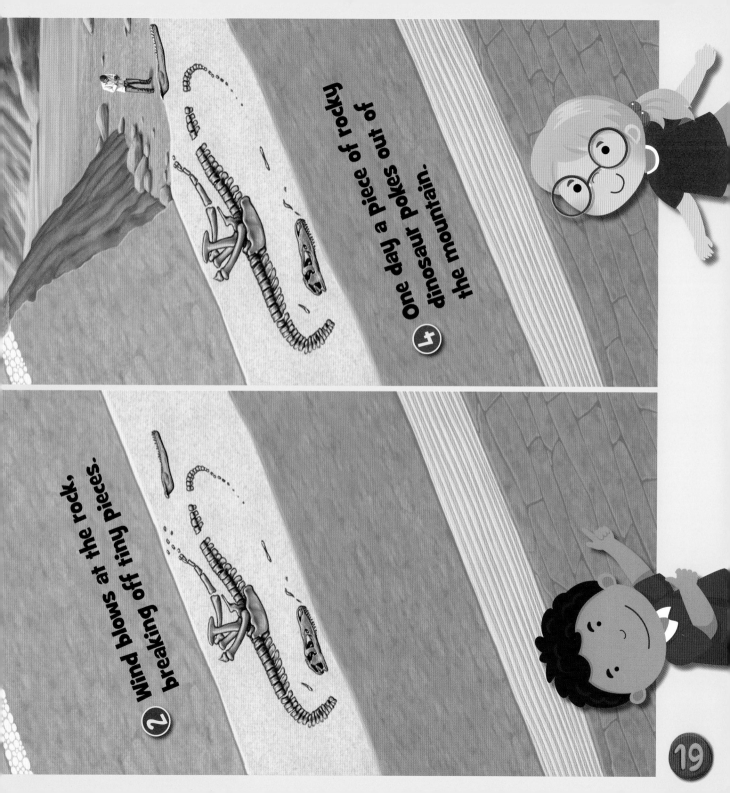

4 One day a piece of rocky dinosaur pokes out of the mountain.

2 Wind blows at the rock, breaking off tiny pieces.

19

Scientists carefully **dig** a **dinosaur skeleton** out of the **rock**.

fossil

rock

A **dinosaur bone** that has turned to **rock** is called a **fossil**.

dinosaur's tail

palaeontologist

A scientist who digs up dinosaurs is called a palaeontologist.

Let's say it!
"pay-lee-on-TOL-uh-gist"

Palaeontologists use these tools.

Palaeontologists have **discovered** about 700 different kinds of **dinosaurs**.

Triceratops

What's this lumpy fossil? It's a prehistoric poo!

It belonged to a dinosaur.

Stegosaurus

The **dinosaurs** are gone, but we can see their **fossils** in **museums.**

Tyrannosaurus rex

Now we know what happened to the dinosaurs.

Good work, little scientists!

23

My Science Words

extinct
No longer alive and gone forever.

fossil
The hard remains of a living thing, such as an animal, that have become rock.

palaeontologist
A scientist who studies animals and plants from long ago.

prehistoric
A time long, long ago before there were people.